ONE HUNDRED PERSONAL PRAYERS OLD AND NEW

GEORGE APPLETON

LUTTERWORTH PRESS

CAMBRIDGE

In grateful remembrance
of
Dean Eric Milner-White
who both practised and taught
a life of prayer

Lutterworth Press
P.O. Box 60
Cambridge CB1 2NT

British Library Cataloguing in Publication Data

100 personal prayers old and new.
1. Prayer-books
I. Appleton, George
242'.8   BV245

ISBN 0-7188-2703-1

First published in the UK 1988 by Lutterworth Press

Printed in Great Britain by
The Guernsey Press Co Ltd, Guernsey,
Channel Islands

CONTENTS

INTRODUCTION

Some of these 100 prayers have come down through the centuries and have been prayed and recorded by prayerful people, until in this twentieth century they have been discovered and prayed and written down for regular use. Such prayers are not new, but they have been new to me and gratefully used. This small book may enable others to discover and pray them in turn.

Other prayers have come out of meditation, rather than composed and then meditated on, and as such I dare to hope that in some mystical way they are evidence of personal experience of and relationship with the Risen Lord, and through him with the Eternal and Universal Father, whom he reveals to us mortals in both his incarnate and risen life.

NEW LESSONS

As my later years go by (b.1902) I am learning the deep truth of our Lord's warning 'they think that they will be heard for their many words'. Introducing this warning, he urges us 'when you pray go into your room and shut the door and pray to your Father who is in secret; and your Father who sees in secret will reward you'. I cannot think that he was referring to a material room with four walls and a door, but to the inmost room of the heart. Nor do I expect material rewards or worldly success as a reward, but the activity of God the Spirit within my being, progressively sanctifying me, making me more holy and loving, until I approach in some measure to the character, maturity and likeness of his perfect Son. St Paul's experience becomes relevant: 'Not that I have already obtained this or am already perfect; but I press on to make it my own because Jesus Christ has made me his own. Brethren, I do not consider that I have made it my own; but one thing I do, forgetting what lies behind and straining forward to what lies ahead. I press on towards the goal for the prize of the upward call of God in Jesus Christ.' (Philippians 3:12–14).

EXPERIENCING GOD

Prayer can be said to consist of getting to know God, personally, intimately, and experientially, not just knowing about God, but a relationship with Him. In his great prayer on the night before Jesus went to the cross, he thanks God for the disciples God has given him, of whom only one has been lost. He tells the Father that he is conscious of the divine authority to give eternal life to all entrusted to his care. Then he adds: 'this is eternal life to know You the only true God'; St John, who is recording years later what he remembers of that last prayer, in all probability added the words 'and Jesus Christ, whom You have sent' (John 17:3). So prayer is our relationship with God and Christ, and any loving relationship requires a mutual opening up of heart and mind, which is not a monologue but a duologue involving listening as well as speaking.

Every time of prayer should include a time of silence equal to the time spent in vocal prayer. In that silence God may speak to the praying soul, and in our time-bound existence it takes some time before what is said by God in the silence becomes translated into thought and then into perception and understanding. I have often found that in praying about some person, situation or problem, this clarity may not come immediately, but when I am engaged on some ordinary activity a crystallised message arises in the conscious mind and I recognise that it is the answer I was seeking to know from God in the time of prayer perhaps the day before.

PREPARING FOR PRAYER

Another lesson that I have learnt over the years is that there should be a time of quiet preparation, when one needs to become aware of the presence of God. The great teachers of prayer, non-Christian as well as Christian, suggest that there are three stages in this preparation. First of all, they say, there needs to be a relaxation of the body, so that there is no rigidity in any limb, no puckering of the brow or tension (for me) in the hands. The second step is the stilling of the mind, the switching off, as it were, of the machinery of thought. It is then possible for the third stage which is the lifting up of the heart to God, the centring of the attention on Him. This third stage requires considerable discipline, for the attention is so easily distracted by the noise of a plane or passing car, a cough from one of the praying companions or just the butterfly character of one's own mind. Every time my attention is distracted I have to bring it back gently but firmly, so that in the end the mind obeys the will.

With that threefold preparation one is ready to pour out the heart to God, to listen to Him and to allow Him to act within the personality which He is creating, guiding and sanctifying. All this sounds like self-effort, and governing the whole spiritual activity is the conviction that God takes the initiative, He comes to us. Our desire for Him, our opening the whole being to Him, our waiting upon Him in love and trust, are all signs of his presence and activity within us.

THE PRAYER OF LOVE

Most British Christians find intercession to be the form of prayer that is most imperative. In earlier years I did intercede for loved ones and suffering ones, but it was very much as a duty, demanding considerable effort. Then one day a trusted friend suggested that if one regarded intercession as the prayer of love it became an exciting and creative activity without losing its sense of neighbourly spiritual duty. A further insight came very soon after that understanding, namely that intercession involved holding loved ones or suffering ones in the loving, healing, strengthening presence of God who is love. In this way intercession became a kind of spiritual X-ray, killing every kind of evil infection of spirit, mind and body. With this inspiration I was somehow led to repeating a number of times the name of anyone, with a pause of some seconds after each mention, not with the aim of reminding or importuning God, but of offering myself as a little human channel for his grace and love, if his own ineffable direct grace was not being consciously perceived and gratefully accepted. In this way I began to think of intercession as a transmitter or even transformer of divine grace and love. I learned also not to begin each successive time of prayer as if God had not responded to the earlier prayers. So when I needed a vocalised remembrance or prayer, the opening words were: 'Continue, dear God, your loving will and care for the one I love, the one You love infinitely more than I do.' Underlying the whole situation should be our Lord's confident assurance that no one or any happening can snatch the prayed-for-ones out of his hand, adding: 'My Father who has given them to me is greater than all, and no one is able to snatch them out of the Father's hand. I and the Father are one.' (John 10:28–30). The sad thing is that so many do not know that they are in the Father's hand, and many of those who do, slip out of that fatherly hand through weakness or deliberate choice.

ALWAYS WITH THANKSGIVING

St Paul added a further facet to prayer. Writing to converts at Philippi he urged: 'Have no anxiety about anything, but in everything by prayer and supplication (i.e. *intercession*) with thanksgiving let your requests be made known to God.' (4:6). Following this advice we should always precede our intercessions with thanksgiving – for what God is, for the revelation of his being, will and love in Jesus, for his love for every soul and particularly for the one for whom we are praying, and for each of us praying.

It perhaps needs saying that we need to have done everything within our own power to answer our own prayers, and to be ready to do anything God puts into our minds. Mark, in his account of the feeding of the crowd on the other side of the lake, tells how when the disciples urged Jesus to send the people away, Jesus replied, 'You give them something to eat', implying that there was some food available. John's gospel adds the interesting detail of the lad with his five small rolls and two fish, who presumably handed them to Jesus for the usual blessing of God before taking food. It is quite possible that others followed the boy's example and brought what they had left to share with those around, until in the end all had been fed, and there were twelve baskets of broken pieces left over, a miracle of unselfish sharing, showing us how world hunger and poverty could be banished, especially if overseas aid enabled people to grow more food in addition to providing immediate compassionate relief.

Prayer takes us over the frontier between this world and the next, and so permits us in God's economy of the Kingdom to keep in spiritual touch with those whom we speak of as having 'died'. It would be more trustful and hopeful to speak of them as 'the risen ones'. Friends with whom I share this thought remind me of the parable of the rich man and Lazarus in which Father Abraham speaks of the great gulf fixed, impassable either way. When he told that parable Jesus had not yet died, but in his death and saving love spanned the great gulf, as well as rending from top to bottom every curtain of separation. In this understanding, when we pray in spirit and truth, we get a foretaste of the Eternal Kingdom and the Divine Milieu.

SOME CONSEQUENCES OF PRAYER

The discipline of prayer which I have tried to interpret, describe and practise has some radical effects in the lives of those whose spiritual eyes are open to perceive the presence and activity of the God whose will is to share his divine life with all whom He has created (2 Peter 1:3–4).

When I am in communion with Him, I begin to experience the tempo of eternity. We live so much under the pressure of human time, that it is good to take a few minutes regularly and let his peace slow down and calm us. If we keep close to Him, if only to touch the hem of his garment, we shall find our spiritual batteries recharged. Nowadays many of us suffer from blood pressure. A regular period of quiet meditation will bring down the level and control rising excitement, impatience and irritability. Schizophrenia can be cured by unifying the personality under the wise and loving will of God. Co-operating with God to get the kind of world He is always working to create brings adventure and challenge to pedestrian or boring lives. And the assurance of his unfailing presence, even if at times we do not feel Him near, can assure Him that at such times we desire and will his will. If He has our will, He knows that He can do anything loving and godlike in us, with us, and through us. His grace, shown in the life, death and everlivingness of his perfect Son, can transform and even transfigure us. Luke in his gospel tells us that Jesus was transfigured before his watching disciples while He was praying. An inner glory shone through the joy on his face as he communed with the Father. Something like that could happen to us. Loving communion with God prepares us for the sphere of the eternal and spiritual. It is a foretaste of the life beyond. We begin to experience eternal life, resurrection life, here and now.

William of Thierry, a contemplative who lived from 1085 to 1148 has left us this fatherland prayer:

> Lord, I am a countryman coming from my country to
> yours.
> Teach me the laws of your country
> its way of life
> its spirit
> So that I feel at home there.

To feel at home with God is the deepest, loveliest, most desirable gift, made possible because God makes his home with us.

AS YOU PRAY THESE PRAYERS

Pause in the opening words of each, lifting the heart in worship to God. After each phrase in each prayer pause again so that it makes its impression on your heart and mind. At the end of each prayer listen for any message which God may be speaking to you, relating to your own life and situation. There will be times when you just don't feel like praying and so be tempted to think that prayer and meditation at such times are of no value. Often it is easy to pray and the heart is warm with the memory of God's goodness or studying Our Lord's way of prayer. To maintain one's discipline and practice of prayer when things are difficult involves the offering and exercise of one's will, and one can be sure that such faithfulness, speaking from the human point of view, will be as pleasing or even more so to God, who knows mind and heart, desire and situation. Spiritual result will be a return, sooner or later, of consciousness of God's presence always and everywhere, and the heart will again be warm with love. On occasions when no word seems to come from God, you may find it helpful to say slowly and thoughtfully in the way already suggested the following prayer:

O God. You have prepared for those who love You and for those who do not yet know and love You such good things as pass our understanding. Pour into our hearts such love for You that we loving You above all things may obtain your promises which exceed all that we desire through Jesus Christ, your beloved Son, our beloved Lord. Amen . . . Amen . . . Amen . . .

George Appleton
Advent 1987

NOTE

All prayers in this collection are by George Appleton except those where another source is indicated.

I

IN THE BEGINNING – GOD

➤ *Beyond all thought* ◄

GOD is what thought cannot better; God is whom thought cannot reach; God no thinking can even conceive. Without God, man can have no being, no reason, no knowledge, no good desire, naught. Thou, O God, art what thou art, transcending all.

Eric Milner-White (1)

➤ *The divine immensity* ◄

O GOD, your immensity fills the earth and the whole universe, but the universe itself cannot contain You, much less the earth, and still less the world of my thoughts.

Father Yves Raguin, SJ (2)

➤➤ *Beyond all images* ◄◄

O THOU, who art beyond all images, thought-forms and word-expressions, have compassion on us who try to express what we have experienced of Thee. We have to think about Thee, picture Thee, speak of Thee; help us to know that we can never grasp Thee but only be grasped by Thee, never describe Thee as object but only experience Thee as subject. Forgive the images that we make of Thee and grant that each successive one may come closer to that given us by thy blessed Son, Jesus Christ our Lord.

(3)

➤➤ *God is all love* ◄◄

O ETERNAL Lord God, I thank You for the revelation of your being, your nature, your will. You are all love, nothing but love, only love comes from You. All that You do to us is loving. You love us when we go astray, You welcome us with unfailing love when we come back home. And You hope that we will begin to love others with the love with which You love us, as shown in your beloved and loving Son, Jesus Christ, our beloved Lord.

(4)

➤➤ *Creator of beauty* ◄◄

LEAD us, O God,
from the sight of the lovely things of the world
to the thought of Thee their Creator;

and grant that delighting
in the beautiful things of thy creation
we may delight in Thee,
the first author of beauty
and the sovereign Lord of all thy works,
blessed for evermore.

(5)

➤➤ *Beyond time and space* ◄◄

O GOD, let me rise to the edges of time and
open my life to your eternity;
let me run to the edges of space and
gaze into your immensity;
let me climb through the barriers of sound
and pass into your silence;
And then, in stillness and silence
let me adore You,
who are Life – Light – Love –
without beginning and without end,
the Source – the Sustainer – the Restorer –
the Purifier – of all that is;
the Lover who has bound earth to heaven
by the beams of a cross;
the Healer who has renewed a dying race
by the blood of a chalice;
the God who has taken man into your glory
by the wounds of sacrifice;
God . . . God . . . God . . . Blessed be God.
Let me adore You.

Sister Ruth, SLG (6)

➤➤ *King of the universe* ◄◄

BLESSED are You, Lord our God, King of the universe. By his word He brings on the evening twilight; in wisdom He opens the gates of dawn, and with foresight makes times pass and seasons change. He sets the stars in the courses in the sky according to his plan. He creates day and night, turning light into darkness and darkness into light. He makes the day fade away and brings on the night, and separates day and night, for He is the Lord of the hosts of heaven. Blessed are You, Lord, who brings on the evening twilight.

Forms of Prayer (Jewish), 1977 (7)

➤➤ *The grace of perception* ◄◄

ALMIGHTY God,
give us wisdom to perceive Thee,
intelligence to understand Thee,
diligence to seek Thee,
patience to wait for Thee,
eyes to behold Thee,
a heart to meditate upon Thee,
and a life to proclaim Thee.

St Benedict (8)

✦ *Opening the heart* ✦

GRANT to me, O Lord, to worship Thee
in spirit and in truth;
to submit all my nature to Thee,
that my conscience may be quickened by thy holiness,
my mind nourished by thy truth,
my imagination purified by thy beauty.
Help me to open my heart to thy love
and to surrender my will to thy purpose.
So may I lift up my heart to Thee
in selfless adoration and love.
Through Jesus Christ my Lord.

(9)

✦ *Words fail* ✦

O THOU supreme! Most secret and most present, most beautiful and strong! What shall I say, my God, my life, my holy joy? What shall any man say when he speaks of Thee?

(10)

➤ *My offering* ◄

LORD,
I offer what I am
to what You are.
I stretch up to You in desire
my attention on You alone.
I cannot grasp You
explain You
describe You
Only cast myself into the depths
of your mystery
Only let your love pierce the
cloud of my unknowing.
Let me forget all but You
You are what I long for
You are my chiefest good
You are my eager hope
You are my allness.

In the glimpses of your eternity
Your unconditioned freedom
Your unfailing wisdom
Your perfect love
I am humble and worshipping
warming to love and hope
waiting and available
for your will
dear Lord.

(11)

II

IN MY BEGINNING

➻ *Before birth* ≺

CREATOR God, I your child, with my inheritance of chromosomes, physical and character-wise, from a long line of ancestors, conceived through the union in love of my parents, developed and guarded in the body of my mother through months of secret growth, with a seed of eternity planted within my being by You, the Original and Eternal Parent of all, Blessed be You for ever.

(12)

➻ *At a baptism* ≺

O GOD, by whose providence human love is permitted to create new life, we want this little one to have your grace throughout his life, his parents to make his home a home of love, his godparents to watch over his true welfare, so that as year follows year, he may be surrounded by love and grow like your perfect Son, blessed by You and a joy to all who know him. We know this is your will for him, O Father of all.

(13)

➤➤ *At a Confirmation* ◄◄

O HOLY Spirit, You know the hearts of these standing before You today. You know what has brought them here. Lord, I think they know their need to be made strong for all the difficulties, temptations, and adventures of life. O Father, may they turn to You at every step and feel the hand of your perfect Son Jesus on their shoulder, accompanying, guiding, blessing them.

(14)

➤ *The adventures of life* ◆

WHEN a knight won his spurs, in the stories of old,
He was gentle and brave, he was gallant and bold;
With a shield on his arm and a lance in his hand
For God and for valour he rode through the land.

No charger have I, and no sword by my side,
Yet still to adventure and battle I ride,
Though back into storyland giants have fled,
And the knights are no more and the dragons are dead.

Let faith be my shield and let joy be my steed
'Gainst the dragons of anger, the ogres of greed;
And let me set free, with the sword of my youth,
From the castle of darkness the power of the truth.

Jan Struther (15)

➤ *Growing in wisdom* ◆

GRANT to me, Lord, to know what I ought to know, to love what I ought to love, to praise what delights You most, to value what is precious in your sight, to hate anything evil as You do. Do not let me judge according to the sight of my eyes, nor pass sentence according to everything I hear, but help me to discern with true judgement between the visible and spiritual, and above all things to enquire what is your good and loving will.

(16)

⤳ *Keeping the childlike heart* ⤳

GRANT me, O God,
the heart of a child,
pure and transparent as a spring;
a simple heart,
which never harbours sorrows;
a heart glorious in self-giving,
tender in compassion;
a heart faithful and generous,
which will never forget any good
or bear a grudge for any evil.

Make me a heart gentle and humble,
loving without asking any return,
largehearted and undauntable,
which no ingratitude can sour
and no indifference can weary;
a heart penetrated by the love of Jesus
whose desire will only be
satisfied in heaven.

Grant me, O Lord,
the mind and heart
of thy dear Son.

(17)

III

EACH DAY

↠ *Every morning* ↞

O ETERNAL Lord God, our Heavenly Father, we have come with You to another day, and offer You at its beginning our gratitude and love. We know that You will defend us today with your protecting power and guide us with your wisdom, so that we fall into no sin nor run into any kind of danger, that all our thinking, speaking and doing may be inspired by your good and loving will. We offer You this prayer as taught by your blessed Son, our beloved Lord.

(18)

✦ *Day by day* ✦

DAY by day,
Dear Lord, of Thee three things I pray:
To see Thee more clearly,
Love Thee more dearly,
Follow Thee more nearly,
Day by day.

St Richard of Chichester (19)

✦ *Daily contacts* ✦

LORD Jesus Christ,
alive and at large in the world,
help me to follow and find you there today,
in the places where I work,
meet people,
spend money
and make plans.
Take me as a disciple of your kingdom,
to see through your eyes,
and hear the questions you are asking,
to welcome all men with your trust and truth
and change the things that contradict God's love
by the power of the cross
and the freedom of your Spirit. Amen.

Bishop John Taylor (20)

➤➤ *Sowing good seeds* ◄◄

MAKE me a good gardener, O Lord.
In the garden of my life,
let me sow seeds of life.
Let my words be good and fruitful.
Let my ideas be sound and fertile.
Let my actions be bright with holiness and love.
As far as lies within my power,
let me sow seeds of thy kingdom,
and do Thou, O Lord of life and growth,
make them germinate and produce
the promised harvest, O Lord of the Hundredfold.

(21)

➤➤ *Work* ◄◄

GOD give me work
till my life shall end,
and life
till my work is done.

Epitaph to Winifred Holtby (22)

➤➤ *Sometimes discouraged* ◄◄

DISCOURAGED in the work of life,
Disheartened by its load,
Shamed by its failures or its fears,
I sink beside the road;
But let me only think of Thee,
And then new heart springs up in me.

S. Longfellow (23)

➤➤ *My sleeping hours* ◀◀

O GOD,
who hast given me such a wonderful nature,
that even when I sleep
my mind continues to think,
giving me understanding of myself
and clues how to live;
help me to know my inner self and to trust it,
for it is there that thy Spirit works.
I praise Thee, my God and Maker,
who dost give gifts to thy loved ones,
even while we sleep.

(24)

➤➤ *Making a stand* ◀◀

LORD, let me stand today –
for whatever is pure and true and just and good;
for the advancement of science and education and true
learning;
for the redemption of daily business from the blight of
self-seeking;
for the rights of the weak and the oppressed;
for industrial co-operation and mutual help;
for the conservation of the rich traditions of the past;
for the recognition of new workings of thy Spirit
in the minds of the men of my own time;
for the hope of yet more glorious days to come;
Lord, let me stand today.

John Baillie (25)

IV

MY NEIGHBOUR

➤➤ *Loved ones* ◄◄

O GOD our Father, we bring before Thee all those whom we love, knowing that Thou dost love them more even than we do and that thy will for them is something better than we can imagine or desire. Let thy will be done in them and for them, and grant them that strength which shall make them more than conquerors, through him who loves them and us, Jesus Christ our Lord.

(26)

➤➤ *Lifetime partner* ◄◄

MAY the God who is Love –
eternally loving –
bless us both
and keep us sweethearts
as we go through life together
in ever-growing tenderness –
until we come hand in hand
to the joyful mystery of Love –
of love eternal and divine.
May the God of Love
bless us both
with love unending.

(27)

➤➤ *Everyone* ◄◄

NOW may every living thing, young or old, weak or
strong, living near or far, known or unknown, living or
departed or yet unborn, may every living thing be full of
bliss.

The Buddha (28)

➤➤ *People of other faith* ◄◄

O SPIRIT of God, guide me
as I seek to discover thy working
with men of other faiths.
Give me the strength of truth,
the gentleness and strength of love,
the clear eye of judgement, and the courage of faith.
Above all, grant me a deeper understanding
of him who is the truth,
a greater commitment to him who is the Lord,
a deeper gratitude to him
who is the Saviour of all,
even Jesus Christ thy eternal word,
through whom Thou art drawing all men
to thyself, that they may be saved for ever,
and worship Thee the only God,
blessed for evermore.

(29)

➤➤ *Even enemies* ◄◄

O LORD, remember not only the men and women of
good will, but also those of ill will. But do not remember
all the suffering they have inflicted on us; remember the
fruits we have bought, thanks to this suffering – our
comradeship, our loyalty, our humility, our courage, our
generosity, the greatness of heart which has grown out
of all this, and when they come to judgement let all the
fruits which we have borne be their forgiveness.

An unknown prisoner (30)

✦ *When protest is right* ✦

O LORD and Saviour Christ, who comest not to strive nor cry, but to let thy words fall as the drops that water the earth; grant to all who contend for the faith once delivered, never to injure it by clamour and impatience; but speaking thy precious truth in love so to present it that it may be loved, and that men may see in it thy goodness and thy beauty . . .

William Bright (31)

✦ *Animals also* ✦

O GOD, I thank Thee
for all the creatures Thou hast made,
so perfect in their kind –
great animals like the elephant and the rhinoceros,
humorous animals like the camel and the monkey,
friendly ones like the dog and the cat,
working ones like the horse and the ox,
timid ones like the squirrel and the rabbit,
majestic ones like the lion and the tiger,
for birds with their songs.
O Lord give us such love for thy creation,
that love may cast out fear,
and all thy creatures see in man
their priest and friend,
through Jesus Christ our Lord.

(32)

⇥ Compassion for all ⇤

GRANT us to look with your eyes of compassion,
O Merciful God, at the long travail of mankind:
the wars, the hungry millions,
the countless refugees,
the natural disasters,
the cruel and needless deaths,
men's inhumanity to one another,
the heartbreak and hopelessness of so many lives.
Hasten the coming of the messianic age
when the nations shall be at peace,
and men shall live free from fear and free from want
and there shall be no more pain or tears,
in the security of your will,
the assurance of your love,
the coming of your kingdom
O God of Righteousness, O Lord of Compassion.

(33)

⇥ The risen ones ⇤

O HEAVENLY Father, who in thy Son Jesus Christ hast
given us a true faith, and a sure hope: Help us, we pray
thee, to live as those who believe and trust in the
communion of saints, the forgiveness of sins, and the
resurrection to life everlasting, and strengthen this faith
and hope in us all the days of our life; through the love of
thy Son, Jesus Christ our Saviour.

Book of Common Prayer, 1928 (34)

V

MY DISCIPLESHIP

There is a spirit in the soul

THERE is a spirit in the soul, untouched by time and flesh, flowing from the spirit, remaining in the spirit, itself wholly spiritual. In this principle is God, ever verdant, ever flowing in all the joy and glory of his actual self. Sometimes I have called that principle the tabernacle of the soul, sometimes a spiritual light, anon I say it is a spark. But now I say it is more exalted over this and that than the heavens are exalted above the earth. So now I name it in a nobler fashion . . . It is free of all names, and void of all forms. It is one and simple as God is one and simple, and no man can in any wise behold it.

Meister Eckhart (35)

⤙ *In the depths* ⤚

HELP me, O Lord, to descend into the depths of my being, below my conscious and subconscious life until I discover my real self, that which is given me from Thee, the divine likeness in which I am made and into which I am to grow, the place where your Spirit communes with mine, the spring from which all my life rises.

(36)

⤙ *Learning to pray* ⤚

LORD, teach me to pray, to want to pray, to delight to pray. When I pray, teach me to pray with faith, with hope, with love. Let me make prayer my first work, my persistent work, my most important work; work that I do for you, for others, for the whole world. Let my prayer be a channel for your love, your grace, your peace for those for whom I pray, and for myself, O dear and blessed Lord.

Eric Milner-White (37)

⤙ *A second language* ⤚

TEACH us, O God, that silent language which says all things. Teach our souls to remain silent in thy presence: that we may adore Thee in the deeps of our being and await all things from Thee, whilst asking of Thee nothing but the accomplishment of thy will. Teach us to remain quiet under thine action and produce in our souls that deep and simple prayer which says nothing and expresses everything, which specifies nothing and includes everything.

Père Grou, SJ (38)

➤➤ *The silence of eternity* ◂◂

O SABBATH rest by Galilee!
O calm of hills above.
Where Jesus knelt to share with Thee
The silence of eternity,
Interpreted by love!

Drop thy still dews of quietness,
Till all our strivings cease;
Take from our souls the strain and stress,
And let our ordered lives confess
The beauty of thy peace.

J.G. Whittier (39)

➤➤ *Following the saints* ◂◂

O GOD, we thank You for the insight of prophets,
apostles and saints that no eye has seen, no ear heard,
nor mind conceived the things You have prepared in
your love for all your created children. In the world of
your eternity time does not limit love, space no longer
separates, no doors or prison bars prevent your entry, no
sin need remain unforgiven. Forgive your child, dear
Father, who tries to think about You and express in
words his experience of You and of your Risen Son,
Jesus Christ my beloved Lord.

(40)

↦ *Quiet hearts* ↤

O SPIRIT of God, set at rest the crowded, hurrying, anxious thoughts within our minds and hearts. Let the peace and quiet of thy presence take possession of us. Help us to rest, to relax, to become open and receptive to Thee. Thou dost know our inmost spirits, the hidden unconscious life within us, the forgotten memories of hurts and fears, the frustrated desires, the unresolved tensions and dilemmas. Cleanse and sweeten the springs of our being, that freedom, life and love may flow into both our conscious and hidden life. Lord, we lie open before Thee, waiting for thy peace, thy healing, and thy word.

(41)

↦ *Not in our strength* ↤

O LORD, we know that we are incompetent to heal ourselves, to sanctify ourselves, to transfigure ourselves. Our holiness is your action in us, through our willingness to accept the indwelling of your Spirit. Heal me, Lord; sanctify me, Lord; transfigure me, Lord; fill me, Lord; direct me, Lord. Use me, Lord.

(42)

➤➤ *Love to all* ◄◄

O THOU source of all love, let thy love go out to all
created beings, to those I love and those who love me, to
the few I know and to the many I do not know, to all of
every race, to all the living in this world and to all the
living dead in the next world: may all be free from evil
and from harm, may all come to know thy love and to
find the happiness of loving Thee and their fellows. O let
the small love of my heart go out with thine all-
embracing love for the sake of him, who first loved us
and taught us love, even Jesus Christ, our Lord.

(43)

➤➤ *Our inmost secrets* ◄◄

ALMIGHTY God, unto whom all hearts be open, all
desires known, and from whom no secrets are hid:
Cleanse the thoughts of our hearts by the inspiration of
thy Holy Spirit, that we may perfectly love thee, and
worthily magnify thy holy name: through Christ our
Lord. Amen.

Book of Common Prayer, 1662 (44)

⤜ *Disciples' school* ⤛

O MY Lord, I realise how far short I fall of your holiness and love. Yet I see in you the perfection which I long to attain. Enrol me in your school that I may learn from you. In your company let me discover how to love and serve my fellow men. Reprove me, train me, encourage me, that at last the disciple may be as his master. Lord and Master, don't despair of me, don't write me off. Without you I am lost, with you there is hope. Lord, there is no other to whom I can go; you have the meaning of life in this world and in the world to come. I am a long way behind, but wherever I see your foot-prints, I will plant my own, straining my eyes to see you far ahead, leading me on to the Father of souls, my Creator and my God.

(45)

⤜ *Divine indwelling* ⤛

O FATHER, I am your child, created by You; let me value my heredity and my heritage. O God, I am answerable to You; let me accept my responsibility to work with You to make the world of your will. O God, I depend on You; give me wisdom, inspiration and staying power. O Eternal One, my life in this world is limited; even now let me live in the dimension of eternity.

(46)

➤➤ *Life support* ◄◄

O MY Lord and God,
the journey is too great for me
unless
You feed me with bread from heaven
and wine of life,
unless
You share with me your own life.

I need, O Father, a transfusion of the spiritual blood
of your Risen Son, flowing through the arteries of my
spirit.
May his strength
be my strength,
his love be my love
and his will my will,
victorious over sin, ill-will,
self-centredness and death.
O Lord, my God,
O Christ, your Son.

(47)

VI

THE WORLD

➤➤ God ever at work ◄◄

O GOD, who hast created the universe and art ever at work in it to restore the harmony broken by the self-will of men: give us quiet, confident, joyful faith in Thee, that our eyes may ever look in expectation to thy love and power, rather than to the power of evil or to the weakness of men. Help us to stand firm in the assurance that Thou art at work in all that happens, in the foolishness and rebellion of men as well as in their efforts for goodness, turning all to thy loving purpose. Fill us with joy and hope in believing, through him who was victorious over sin, enmity, defeat, and death, even Jesus Christ, our beloved Lord.

(48)

⤜ *For all in authority* ⤛

O FATHER of the just, do Thou of thine infinite goodness direct the hearts of all who bear authority. Help them with the power of thy Holy Spirit to make laws in accordance with thy will, and for the advancement of righteousness. Protect them from the snares of the enemy and the deceits of the world; let no pride of power betray them into rejection of thy commandments; and grant that both rulers and people may with one mind serve Thee our God and King, through Jesus Christ. Amen.

Acts of Devotion (49)

⤜ *The world's work* ⤛

O GOD, who givest to every man his work and through his labours dost accomplish thy purpose upon earth: Grant thy blessing, we beseech Thee, to those who are engaged in the industries and commerce of each land. Inspire them with the knowledge that in ministering to the needs of others they are serving Thee; defend them from injustice and greed, and give them the due reward of their labours; that, seeking first thy kingdom and righteousness, all things may be added unto them here and hereafter; through Jesus Christ our Lord.

Acts of Devotion (50)

⤜ *Public opinion* ⤛

ALMIGHTY God, who hast proclaimed thine eternal truth by the voice of prophets and evangelists: Direct and bless, we beseech Thee, those who in this our generation speak where many listen and write what many read; that they may do their part in making the heart of the people wise, its mind sound, and its will righteous; to the honour of Jesus Christ our Lord.

The Book of Common Order (51)

⤜ *The world's peace* ⤛

MAY the memory of two world wars strengthen
our efforts for peace.
May the memory of those who died inspire our
service to the living.
May the memory of past destruction move us to
build for the future.
May the first two atomic bombs be
the last two also.
May the first two world wars be also
the last world wars.
O God of peace,
O Father of souls,
O Builder of the Kingdom of Love.

(52)

➤➤ *Rejecting violence* ◄◄

WE pray that all our fellow human beings may grow in respect for human dignity and its inalienable rights; may we use our own liberty with scrupulous care not to infringe the rights of others, having a practical concern for their needs and facing conflicts with mutual respect and understanding.

> Prayed at the Assisi conference of leaders of world religions,
> October 1986 (53)

➤➤ *Uniting nations* ◄◄

LORD of the Nations, Creator, Redeemer and Father of all men, we thank Thee for the vision of thy purpose to gather all nations into a commonwealth of brotherhood, peace and justice. We thank Thee, All-ruling and Eternal God, for the United Nations Organisation with its aim to eradicate war and reduce armaments, with its service in production of food, its promotion of education and health, its care of refugees and children. Guide all the nations and their leaders, we pray Thee, into deeper unity, greater efforts for peace, more generous contributions to human needs, that men may live free from fear and free from want, and help build the universe of thy love, O God and Father of all.

(54)

➤➤ *Our crowded roads* ◄◄

ALMIGHTY God, giver of life and health, guide, we pray Thee, with thy wisdom all who are striving to save

from injury and death the travellers on our roads. Grant
to those who drive along the highways consideration for
others, and to those who walk on them or play beside
them thoughtful caution and care; that so without fear or
disaster we all may come safely to our journey's end, by
thy mercy who carest for us; through Jesus Christ our
Lord.

(55)

⇥ *Footmarks ahead* ⇤

GUIDE our feet into the way of peace,
for in our confusion we do not know which way to turn;
in the babel of voices we hear no clear word;
in the mass of propaganda we cannot find the truth.
Give us direction in which to move, and when we cannot
find it
guide our feet by thy wisdom, if unperceived by our
understanding.
Keep our hearts peaceful in trust;
give us quiet courage;
keep us steady under criticism or opposition,
with unfailing love towards all, and eager
expectation to see the footmarks of thy dear Son
ahead, perhaps only a step or two, but pointing
to the peace of thy will,
O Creator and Redeemer of all.

(56)

⤞ *Eternal values* ⤝

DELIVER us, O God, from following the fashions of the day in our thinking. Save us from the worship of power, whether power over nature or power over man; save us from the worship of science, and grant that, giving Thee thanks for the skill of the scientist, we may be preserved from the abuse of his discoveries. Help us never to confuse any creature with the Creator, or man with God. May we acknowledge man's reason as thy gift, and being freed from all false hopes and misplaced trust, find in Thee our hope and our salvation, through Jesus Christ our Lord.

Acts of Devotion (57)

⤞ *Into God's hands* ⤝

INTO thy hands, our Father, we commit this thy world, this thy family, for which our Lord Jesus Christ was content to be betrayed, and to suffer death upon the cross. Into thy hands we commit thy Universal Church and her unity. Into thy hands we commit all the problems which seem insoluble, in sure and certain hope; for in Thee is our trust. Here and now we lay all in thy hands. All love, all glory, be unto Thee for ever and ever.

Acts of Devotion (58)

VII

THE CHURCH

→ Christ's collective body ←

O LORD, let the Church be truly your collective body in the world today, the Christ-community directed by you its head, infused with your spirit, loving and serving men as you did when you lived our human life. Help the Church to give itself for the world, so that men may have the priceless treasure of your grace and love, O Lord of the Church, O Saviour of the world.

(59)

➤➤ *Thanksgiving for the Church* ◄◄

O GOD, I thank thee for the Church of thy dear Son,
without which I would not know of thy love;
without which I would not be caught up in worship;
without which I would be lonely and afraid;
without which I would not know of forgiveness and
grace;
without which I would not be constantly reminded
that I am thy child, called to live the Christ-life.
I pray for the Church, that it may be one according to thy
will;
that it may be holy in all its members and in all its
branches;
that it may be catholic – for all men and in all truth;
that it may be apostolic in faith and in outgoing love.
O God, make the Church truly the Body of thy Son,
a community of love and service, a pioneer of salvation.

(60)

➤➤ *Holiness for the Church* ◄◄

MOST gracious Father, we humbly beseech Thee for
thy Holy Catholic Church. Fill it with all truth; in all
truth with all peace. Where it is corrupt, purge it; where
it is in error, direct it; where anything is amiss, reform it;
where it is right, strengthen and confirm it; where it is in
want, furnish it; where it is divided and rent asunder,
make up the breaches of it, O Thou Holy One of Israel.

Archbishop William Laud (61)

➤➤ *Our own Church* ◂◂

PROSPER the labours of all Churches bearing the name of Christ and striving to further righteousness and faith in Him. Help us to place thy truth above our conception of it and joyfully to recognise the presence of the Holy Spirit wherever He may choose to dwell among men. Teach us wherein we are sectarian in our intentions, and give us grace humbly to confess our fault to those whom in past days our communion has driven from its fellowship by ecclesiastical tyranny, spiritual barrenness or moral inefficiency, that we may become worthy and competent to bind up in the Church the wounds of which we are guilty, and hasten the day when there shall be one fold under one Shepherd, Jesus Christ our Lord.

Bishop Brent (62)

➤➤ *Every Church* ◂◂

FATHER, we pray Thee to fill this house with thy Spirit. Here may the strong renew their strength and seek for their working lives a noble consecration. Here may the poor find succour and the friendless friendship. Here may the tempted find power, the sorrowing comfort and the bereaved find the truth that death hath no dominion over their beloved. Here let the fearing find a new courage and the doubting have their faith and hope confirmed. Here may the careless be awakened and all that are oppressed be freed. Hither may many be drawn by thy love and go hence, their doubts resolved and faith renewed, their sins forgiven and their hearts aflame with thy love. Through Jesus Christ our Lord.

From the chapel porch of Pleshey Retreat House (63)

⤛ *Mission to the world* ⤜

SPIRIT of promise, Spirit of unity, we thank Thee that Thou art also the Spirit of renewal. Renew in the whole Church, we pray Thee, that passionate desire for the coming of thy kingdom which will unite all Christians in one mission to the world. May we grow up together into him who is our head, the Saviour of the world, and our only Lord and Master.

Olive Wyon (64)

⤛ *Paul's prayer for the Church* ⤜

FOR this reason I bow my knees before the Father, from whom every family in heaven and on earth is named, that according to the riches of his glory he may grant you to be strengthened with might through his Spirit in the inner man, and that Christ may dwell in your hearts through faith; that you, being rooted and grounded in love, may have power to comprehend with all the saints what is the breadth and length and height and depth, and to know the love of Christ which surpasses knowledge, that you may be filled with all the fullness of God.

St Paul (65)

VIII

SUFFERING

✦ *The mystery of suffering* ✦

O LORD, we pray Thee for all who are weighed down with the mystery of suffering. Reveal thyself to them as the God of love who Thyself dost bear all our sufferings. Grant that they may know that suffering borne in fellowship with Thee is not waste or frustration, but can be turned to goodness and blessing, something greater than if they had never suffered, through him who on the cross suffered rejection and hatred, loneliness and despair, agonising pain and physical death, and rose victorious from the dead, conquering and to conquer, even Jesus Christ our Lord.

(66)

➤➤ *For all in pain* ◄◄

GRANT, O Lord, to all those who are bearing pain, thy spirit of healing, thy spirit of peace and hope, of courage and endurance. Cast out from them the spirit of anxiety and fear; grant them perfect confidence and trust in Thee, that in thy light they may see light; through Jesus Christ our Lord.

Acts of Devotion (67)

➤➤ *A sufferer's prayer* ◄◄

O HOLY Blessed and Glorious Trinity, accept the praise due to Thee from the heart of this thy child. With my service of praise I offer Thee thanksgiving for all Thou art to me; Father, Saviour and Sanctifier; my Creator, Redeemer and Source of Love. In deepest reverence I offer the remainder of my life to Thee to use as Thou dost will; I pray that Thou wilt accept each day as lived for love of Thee, and to the praise of thy glory. This I offer in Jesu's Name with the aspiration that I keep true to Thee to the end of my life for his sake, whose example I would humbly follow now and always. Amen.

Edith Barfoot (68)

⇥ *For the sick in mind* ⇤

O HOLY Spirit, who dost search out all things, even the deep things of God and the deep things of man: We pray Thee so to penetrate into the springs of personality of all who are sick in mind, to bring them cleansing, healing, and unity. Sanctify all memory, dispel all fear, and bring them to love Thee with all their mind and will, that they may be made whole and glorify Thee for ever. We ask this in the name of him who cast out devils and healed men's minds, even Jesus Christ our Lord.

(69)

⇥ *For a suicide* ⇤

O GOD, righteous and compassionate
Forgive the despair of . . . . . for whom we pray.
Heal in her that which is broken
and in your great Love stand with those
hurt by the violence of her end.
Lord, be to her not a Judge but a Saviour.
Receive her into that Kingdom wherein by your mercy
we sinners also would have place
through the merits of our wounded Redeemer
who lives and reigns with you in the Holy Spirit's power
now and unto the Ages of Ages. Amen.

From the Sisters of the Love of God (70)

⤛ *Diseases at present incurable* ⤜

O HEAVENLY Father, we pray Thee for those suffering from diseases for which at present there is no cure.
Give them the victory of trust and hope, that they may
never lose their faith in thy loving purpose. Grant thy
wisdom to all who are working to discover the causes of
disease, and the realisation that through Thee all things
are possible. We ask this in the Name of him who went
about doing good and healing all manner of disease,
even thy Son Jesus Christ our Lord.

Acts of Devotion (71)

⤛ *A late night prayer* ⤜

WATCH Thou, O Lord, with those who wake, or
watch, or weep tonight, and give thine angels charge
over those who sleep. Tend thy sick ones, O Lord
Christ; rest thy weary ones; bless thy dying ones; soothe
thy suffering ones; pity thine afflicted ones; shield thy
joyous ones. And all, for thy love's sake.

St Augustine (72)

IX

GROWING OLD

⟶ *Signs of age* ⟵

WHEN the signs of age begin to mark my body (and still more when they touch my mind); when the ill that is to diminish me or carry me off strikes from without or is born within me; when the painful moment comes in which I suddenly awaken to the fact that I am ill or growing old; and above all at that last moment when I feel that I am losing hold of myself and am absolutely passive within the hands of the great unknown forces that have formed me; in all those dark moments, O God, grant that I may understand that it is You (provided only my faith is strong enough) who are painfully parting the fibres of my being in order to penetrate to the very marrow of my substance and bear me away within Yourself.

Teilhard de Chardin, SJ (73)

➤➤ *Looking back* ◄◄

LOOKING back on my journey so far, dear Lord, I see how your love and goodness have been with me, through many failings and dangers, in many joys and adventures. I have received much love from friends, been guided and inspired by the wisdom and encouragement of many teachers and writers. Often I have felt your presence near, and sometimes I have had to walk by faith. Forgive my slowness, my failures in faith, the smallness of my love, my poor use of your grace. Accept my heart's thanks for growing knowledge of You, for increasing assurance of your loving purpose and deepening understanding of the things that are eternal. As I turn again to the journey ahead, it is bright with the remembrances of past mercies, O dear and gracious Father and Saviour.

(74)

➤➤ *Anniversaries* ◄◄

GRANT, O Lord, that the years that are left may be the holiest, the most loving, the most mature. I thank You for the past and especially that You have kept the good wine until now, as if it is a jubilee. Help me to accept diminishing powers as the opportunity to prepare my soul for the full and free life. You made known and possible through your beloved Son, Jesus Christ our beloved Lord.

(75)

➻ *Looking forward* ➺

THERE will come a time when my links with earth will grow weaker, when my powers fail, when I must bid farewell to dear ones still rooted in this life with their tasks to fulfil and their loved ones to care for, when I must detach myself from the loveliest things and begin the lonely journey. Then I shall hear the voice of my beloved Christ, saying 'It is I, be not afraid'. So with my hand in his, from the seemingly dark valley I shall see the shining City of God and climb with quiet trusting steps and be met by the Father of souls and clasped in the everlasting arms.

(76)

➻ *Still lovelier* ➺

O GOD, grant that I may go on exchanging pearls for pearls, small truths for greater truths, good things for better things, until I come at length to the Truth itself, to Thee who art its source and giver, the giver of all good and the source of all love.

(77)

➤➤ *The gateway to life* ◄◄

MAY the Father bless them, who created all things in the
beginning; may the Son of God heal them; may the Holy
Spirit enlighten them, guard their bodies, save their
souls, direct their thoughts, and bring them safe to the
heavenly country, where Father, Son, and Holy Spirit
ever reign, one God blessed for evermore.

(78)

➤➤ *The Church's commendation* ◄◄

GO forth upon thy journey from this world,
O Christian soul,
in the name of God the Father Almighty
who created thee;
in the name of Jesus Christ who suffered for thee;
in the name of the Holy Ghost who strengtheneth thee;
in communion with the blessed Saints,
and aided by Angels and Archangels,
and all the armies of the heavenly host.
May thy portion this day be in peace, and thy dwelling in
the heavenly Jerusalem. Amen.

Traditional (79)

➻ *A final offering* ➺

ON the day when death will knock at my door what shall I offer him, either in the closing minutes of this life or in the opening minutes of my new birth in the life beyond? Oh, I will set before him all the lovely things that I have seen, all the love that I have received and given, all the insights of truth that I have gathered, all the things that I have valued and enjoyed, all the tasks completed or left for others, all my gratitude and love for the past, all my content in the present and my hope for the future. Above all I will offer my recognition of the Lord who has come in the guise of death, to lead me to the home he has prepared for me.

(80)

X

THROUGH JESUS CHRIST

➤ *The mind of Christ* ◄

O CHRIST my Lord, let me have your mind, the priority in all your thinking of the Father, the intention to do the things which the Father is always willing, the quiet trust that the final result is in his hand. O Everlasting One, show me how you lived when you were here in the flesh and how you would live in our complex days of pressure and noise and wider community. Give me your mind for life today and tomorrow and all my days.

(81)

➤ *Without Christ* ◄

O LORD Jesus Christ, without you I would not have known the limitless love of God. Without you I would not have known the extent of God's forgiveness or seen it in operation on the cross. Without your rescue I would still be submerged in weakness and sin. Without you I would not have the divine grace to transform my life. Without you I would not have known of the Kingdom of God or our Father's plan to unite humanity in righteousness and love. I can never thank you enough, or love you enough, my Redeemer and the Saviour of the world.

(82)

➤➤ *Thanksgiving for the cross* ◀◀

BLESSED be thy name, O Jesu, Son of the most high God; blessed be the sorrow thou sufferedst when thy holy hands and feet were nailed to the tree; and blessed thy love when, the fullness of pain accomplished, thou didst give thy soul into the hands of the Father; so by thy cross and precious blood redeeming all the world, all longing souls departed and the numberless unborn; who now livest and reignest in the glory of God for ever and ever.

Eric Milner-White (83)

⤜ *Crucified with Christ* ⤛

O GOD our Father, help us to nail to the cross of thy
dear Son the selfish nature, the wrong desires of the
heart, the sinful devisings of the mind, the corrupt
apprehensions of the eyes, the cruel words of the tongue,
the ill employment of hands and feet; that the old nature
being crucified and done away, our new being may live
and grow into the glorious likeness of thy dear Son Jesus
Christ; who liveth and reigneth with Thee and the Holy
Ghost, one God, world without end.

Eric Milner-White (84)

⤜ *All God's people* ⤛

ETERNAL God, whose image lies in the hearts of all
people,
We live among peoples whose ways are different from
ours,
whose faiths are foreign to us,
whose tongues are unintelligible to us.
Help us to remember that You love all people with your
great love,
that all religion is an attempt to respond to You,
that the yearnings of other hearts are much like our own
and are known to You.
Help us to recognise You in the words of truth, the
things of beauty, the actions of love about us.
We pray through Christ, who is a stranger to no one
land more than another, and to every land no less than to
another.

World Council of Churches (85)

➵ *A new world* ➴

O ETERNAL God, with thy life within me I am transformed, with quiet trust, with growing love, seeing life as a joyful adventure. I look out on the world through new eyes, seeing wonder and beauty in every created thing. I see my fellow men no longer as rivals for the things I want or obstacles to my own advancement but as friends and brothers. I see death as my final birth into the sphere of the eternal, which I have already glimpsed and tasted through my touch with Thee, O Blessed and Beloved One.

(86)

➵ *Only Now* ➴

O LORD God, I know how far short I fall of your perfection, holiness and love. Only as I become more conscious of your presence in the depth of my being shall I begin to grow like your perfect Son Jesus Christ who has revealed to all believers your nature, will and saving grace. O God, Father of all, his Father and my Father. Father, dear Father!

(87)

➻ *O Thou who camest from above* ➺

O THOU who camest from above,
The pure celestial fire to impart,
Kindle a flame of sacred love
On the mean altar of my heart.

Jesus, confirm my heart's desire
To work, and speak, and think for thee;
Still let me guard the holy fire,
And still stir up thy gift in me.

Ready for all thy perfect will,
My acts of faith and love repeat,
Till death thy endless mercies seal,
And make my sacrifice complete.

Charles Wesley (88)

➻ *Shepherd of souls* ➺

NOW may the God of peace who brought again from
the dead our Lord Jesus, the great shepherd of the sheep,
by the blood of the eternal covenant, equip you with
everything good that you may do his will, working in
you that which is pleasing in his sight, through Jesus
Christ; to whom be glory for ever and ever. Amen.

Hebrews 13:20–21 (89)

XI

IN THE END – GOD

➤ *Before the end* ◄

WE are all mortal, O Lord,
and our future lies with Thee.
Make us so conscious of Thee that death may be
no break but a new dimension of being,
better than anything so far.
Help us to leave no duty undone,
no sin unrepented,
no relationship unsanctified,
and grant us the faith that the best is yet to be.
So let us live in hope and love
and joyful expectation,
without fear and without regret,
knowing Thee to be the God and Father of
Jesus Christ, and our Father, and
the God and Father of all.

↠ *Over the horizon* ↞

WE give back to You, O God, those whom You gave to us. You did not lose them when You gave them to us, and we do not lose them by their return to You. Your dear Son has taught us that life is eternal and love cannot die. So death is only an horizon, and an horizon is only the limit of our sight. Open our eyes to see more clearly, and draw us closer to You that we may know that we are nearer to our loved ones, who are with You. You have told us that You are preparing a place for us: prepare us also for that happy place, that where You are we may also be always, O dear Lord of life and death.

William Penn (91)

↠ *Christ's Third Coming* ↞

LET me love thee, O Christ,
in thy first coming,
when thou wast made man, for love of man,
and for love of me.

Let me love thee, O Christ
in thy second coming,
when with an inconceivable love
thou standest and knockest at the door,
and wouldest enter into the souls of men,
and into mine.

Plant in my soul, O Christ, thy likeness of love;
that when by death thou callest,
it may be ready,
and burning,
to come unto thee.

Eric Milner-White (92)

➤➤ *Reunion* ◅◅

GRANT unto us, O God, to trust Thee not for ourselves
alone, but for those also whom we love and who are hid
from us by the shadow of death; that, as we believe thy
power to have raised our Lord Jesus Christ from the
dead, so we may trust thy love to give eternal life to all
who believe in him; through the same Jesus Christ our
Lord.

Acts of Devotion (93)

➤➤ *Journey's end* ◅◅

O FATHER, give the spirit power to climb
to the fountain of all light, and be purified.
Break through the mists of earth, the weight of the clod.
Shine forth in splendour, Thou that art calm weather,
and quiet resting place for faithful souls.
To see Thee is the end and the beginning.
Thou carriest us, and Thou dost go before.
Thou art the journey, and the journey's end.

Boethius (94)

↦ *Into the presence* ↤

ETERNAL Light, shine into our hearts.
Eternal Goodness, deliver us from evil.
Eternal Power, be our support,
Eternal Wisdom, scatter the darkness of our ignorance.
Eternal Pity, have mercy upon us;
that with all our heart and mind and soul and
strength we may seek thy face and be brought by
thine infinite mercy to thy holy presence; through
Jesus Christ our Lord.

Alcuin (95)

↦ *God's new order* ↤

O GOD of Eternity and Creator of time, we know that
each generation has to learn afresh of what Thou hast
done in the past and receive from the passing generation
the heritage of faith. Grant that each succeeding generation may take its part in the unfinished task of establish-
ing thy kingdom, keeping alight the torch of faith and
receiving from Thee grace to prepare for the new order
of being which Thou hast prepared for us in they Son,
Jesus Christ, our ever-living Lord.

(96)

⤞ *'I will lift up my eyes'* ⤝

ALMIGHTY and Everlasting God, who hast set thine eternity in our hearts and awakened within us desires which the world cannot satisfy: Lift our eyes, we pray thee, above the narrow horizons of this present world, that we may behold the things eternal in the heaven, wherein is laid up for us an inheritance that fadeth not away; through Jesus Christ our Lord.

George W. Briggs (97)

⤞ *'Abide with us'* ⤝

ABIDE with us, O Lord, for it is toward evening and the day is far spent: Abide with us, and with thy whole Church. Abide with us in the evening of the day, in the evening of life, in the evening of the world. Abide with us in thy grace and mercy, in holy Word and Sacrament, in thy comfort and thy blessing. Abide with us in the night of distress and fear, in the night of doubt and temptation, in the night of death, when these shall overtake us. Abide with us and with all thy faithful ones, O Lord, in time and in eternity.

Lutheran Manual of Prayer (98)

⤙ *In thy house for ever* ⤚

YEA, though I walk through the valley of the shadow of death, I will fear no evil: For Thou art with me; thy rod and thy staff comfort me. Thou shalt prepare a table before me against them that trouble me: Thou hast anointed my head with oil, and my cup shall be full.

Psalm 23:4–5 (99)

⤙ *At the end – God* ⤚

THERE in that other world, what waits for me?
What shall I find after that new birth?
No stormy, tossing, frowning, smiling sea,
But a new earth.

No sun to mark the changing of the days,
No slow, soft falling of the alternate night,
No morn, no stars, no light upon my ways,
Only the light.

No grey cathedral, wide and wondrous fair,
That I may tread where all my fathers trod.
Nay, nay, my soul, no house of God is there,
But only God!

Mary Coleridge (100)

A NOTE ON SOURCES

⤜ *I In the beginning – God* ⤛

1. Eric Milner-White, Dean of King's College, Cambridge and later Dean of York Minster, *My God My Glory* (SPCK).
2. Father Yves Raguin, SJ, quoted in *The Oxford Book of Prayer* (OUP).
3. George Appleton, *Journey for a Soul* (Collins).
4. George Appleton.
5. George Appleton, based on *Wisdom*, 13:1–9 (RSV).
6. Sister Ruth, Sisters of the Love of God, quoted in *The Oxford Book of Prayer* (OUP).
7. *Forms of Prayer* (Jewish).
8. St Benedict (480–543).
9. George Appleton, based on a paragraph in William Temple, *Readings in St John's Gospel* (Macmillan).
10. St Augustine of Hippo (354–430), quoted in George Appleton, *Journey for a Soul* (Collins).
11. George Appleton.

⇥ *II In my beginning* ⇤

12. George Appleton.
13. George Appleton, *Journey for a Soul* (Collins).
14. George Appleton, *Prayers from a Troubled Heart* (DLT).
15. Jan Struther, *Songs of Praise* 377 (OUP).
16. George Appleton, inspired by a prayer of Thomas à Kempis (1380–1471).
17. George Appleton, from a French prayer discovered in a retreat at an ecumenical centre.

⇥ *III Each day* ⇤

18. George Appleton, based on a collect in the *Book of Common Prayer*.
19. St Richard of Chichester (1197–1253), *Songs of Praise* 399 (OUP).
20. Bishop John Taylor, prayed at his enthronement as Bishop of Winchester.
21. George Appleton, *One Man's Prayers* (SPCK).
22. Engraved on the tombstone of Winifred Holtby, novelist (1898–1935).
23. S. Longfellow (1819–92), *Songs of Praise* 532 (OUP).
24. George Appleton, *One Man's Prayers* (SPCK).
25. John Baillie, quoted in George Appleton, *Acts of Worship* (SPCK).

⇥ *IV My neighbour* ⇤

26. George Appleton, *Daily Prayer and Praise* (Lutterworth).
27. George Appleton.
28. The Buddha.
29. George Appleton, *One Man's Prayers* (SPCK).
30. Written by an unknown prisoner in Ravensbrück Concentration Camp and left by the body of a dead child.

31. William Bright (1824–1901), *Ancient Collects*.
32. George Appleton, *One Man's Prayers* (SPCK).
33. ibid.
34. *Book of Common Prayer*, 1928.

⇥ *V My discipleship* ⇤

35. Meister Eckhart (1260–1327), a German Dominican mystic,
    quoted in George Appleton, *Journey for a Soul* (Collins).
36. George Appleton, *One Man's Prayers* (SPCK).
37. Eric Milner-White, *My God My Glory* (adapted) (SPCK).
38. Père Grou, SJ (1731–1803), quoted in George Appleton, *The
    Practice of Prayer* (Mowbray).
39. J.G. Whittier (1807–92), *Songs of Praise* 481 (OUP).
40. George Appleton.
41. George Appleton, *Journey for a Soul* (Collins).
42. George Appleton.
43. ibid.
44. *Book of Common Prayer*, 1662.
45. George Appleton, *Journey for a Soul* (Collins).
46. George Appleton.
47. George Appleton, *One Man's Prayers* (SPCK).

⇥ *VI The world* ⇤

48. George Appleton.
49. Anon, quoted in *Acts of Devotion*, George Appleton (SPCK).
50. *Acts of Devotion*, George Appleton.
51. *The Book of Common Order* (Church of Scotland).
52. George Appleton.
53. Prayed at Assisi in October 1986 at the Conference of leaders
    of world religions, called by Pope John Paul II.
54. George Appleton.
55. George Appleton.
56. George Appleton, *Jerusalem Prayers* (SPCK).

57. Quoted in *Acts of Devotion*, George Appleton.
58. Probably Olive Wyon, quoted also in *Acts of Devotion*.

➤➤ *VII The church* ◄◄

59. George Appleton, *Journey for a Soul* (Collins).
60. George Appleton, *One Man's Prayers* (SPCK).
61. Archbishop William Laud (1573–1645), quoted in *Daily Prayer and Praise* (Lutterworth).
62. Bishop Brent of the USA (1862–1929) quoted in *The Oxford Book of Prayer* (OUP).
63. From the chapel porch of Pleshey Retreat House, for many years the spiritual centre of Evelyn Underhill (1875–1941).
64. Olive Wyon (1881–1966) from a card of prayers for unity, published by the Conference of British Missionary Societies.
65. St Paul's prayer for the Church in *Ephesians* 3:14–19.

➤➤ *VIII Suffering* ◄◄

66. George Appleton, *Journey for a Soul* (Collins).
67. *Acts of Devotion*, George Appleton (SPCK).
68. A prayer of Edith Barfoot, quoted with permission from Sir Basil Blackwell who described her sufferings in a very moving book, published by the firm he founded.
69. George Appleton.
70. Included with the permission of the Sisters of the Love of God, Fairacres, Oxford.
71. George Appleton, *Acts of Devotion* (SPCK).
72. St Augustine of Hippo (354–430).

➤➤ *IX Growing old* ◄◄

73. Teilhard de Chardin, SJ, *Le Milieu Divin* (Collins).
74. George Appleton.

75. George Appleton, *Jerusalem Prayers* (SPCK).
76. George Appleton, *Journey for a Soul* (Collins).
77. ibid.
78. ibid.
79. Traditional.
80. George Appleton, inspired by Rabindranath Tagore.

⤞ X *Through Jesus Christ* ⤝

81. George Appleton, *Journey for a Soul* (Collins).
82. ibid.
83. Dean Milner-White, *A Procession of Passion Prayers* (SPCK).
84. ibid.
85. World Council of Churches, Vancouver Assembly 1983.
86. George Appleton, *Journey for a Soul* (Collins).
87. George Appleton.
88. Charles Wesley (1707–85), *English Hymnal* 343.
89. Hebrews 13:20–21.

⤞ XI *In the end – God* ⤝

90. George Appleton, *Entry into Life* (DLT).
91. William Penn (1644–1718).
92. Dean Milner-White, *My God My Glory* (SPCK).
93. *Acts of Devotion* edited by George Appleton, Gollancz (SPCK).
94. Boethius (480–524), translated by Helen Waddell in *More Latin Lyrics,* edited by Dame Felicitas Corrigan, OSB (Gollancz).
95. Alcuin (735–804), quoted in *Daily Prayer*, a collection of prayers by Dean Milner-White and Canon George W. Briggs.
96. George Appleton, *In His Name* (Lutterworth).
97. George W. Briggs in *The Prayer Manual*, edited by Frederick B. Macnutt (Mowbray).
98. *Lutheran Manual of Prayer.*
99. Psalm 23:4–5.
100. Mary Coleridge (1861–1907), in *The Faber Book of Religious Verse*, edited by Helen Gardner.

INDEX OF FIRST LINES

ACKNOWLEDGEMENTS

The author and publisher would like to thank the following for their permission to use the following prayers in this anthology: 1, 37, 92, SPCK from *My God My Glory* by Eric Milner-White; 2, Anthony Clarke Books from *Paths of Contemplation*; 3, 35, 41, 45, 59, 66, 76, 77, 78, 81, 82, 86, Wm Collins & Sons Ltd from *Journey for a Soul* by George Appleton; 6, Sister Ruth SLG; 9, Oxford University Press from *Enlarged Songs of Praise* by Jan Struther (1901–53); 14, Darton, Longman & Todd from *Prayers from a Troubled Heart* by George Appleton; 20, Bishop John V. Taylor; 21, 24, 29, 32, 33, 47, 60, SPCK from *One Man's Prayers* by George Appleton; 25, SPCK from *Acts of Worship* by George Appleton; 34, Central Board of Finance of the Church of England from the Prayer Book as proposed in 1928; 44, Extract from the *Book of Common Prayer* (1662), the rights of which are vested in the Crown in perpetuity with in the United Kingdom, are reproduced by permission of Eyre & Spottiswoode Publishers, Her Majesty's Printers, London; 49, 50, 57, 58, 67, 71, 93, SPCK from *Acts of Devotion* by George Appleton; 51, Reproduced by kind permission of the General Assembly's panel on Worship from the *Book of Common Order* (1979) published by St Andrew's Press, Edinburgh; 56, 75, SPCK from *Jerusalem Prayers* by George Appleton; 64, Olive Wyon; 70, Reverend V Stock; 73, Wm Collins & Sons Ltd from *Le Milieu Divin* by Teilhard de Chardin, SJ; 83, 84, SPCK from *A Procession of Passion Prayers* by Eric Milner-White; 90, Darton Longman & Todd from *Entry into Life* by George Appleton;

Every attempt has been made to trace the copyright on all works reproduced in this publication. If any copyright has been unwittingly transgressed, or a necessary gratitude gone unexpressed, the author and publisher offer their sincere apologies and will rectify any such oversight in future editions.